T0196685

Lillies of Hope

AMY RUPPEL

authorHOUSE®

AuthorHouse™
1663 Liberty Drive
Bloomington, IN 47403
www.authorhouse.com
Phone: 1-800-839-8640

Published by AuthorHouse   2/2/2012

ISBN: 978-1-4685-3710-9 (sc)
ISBN: 978-1-4685-3709-3 (e)

Library of Congress Control Number: 2012900197

I *was* *in* *awe* *and* wonderment of her and soaked in all her beauty. I held her with all the tenderness and love I had. I wrapped her in the blanket of warm love and kept her close to me.

I had no idea of the future but looked forward to whatever it was.

We were all so pleased and joyed she was here with us.

She was so beautiful, and precious. I tended to her day and night and hoped and prayed I was doing it right.

This is a story about an angel who flew into my life and stayed just long enough to spread love and joy like no one else ever could. Stayed to care for those who needed her and left an impression unlike no other.

She inspired us and left us with a feeling in our heart as if an angel had kissed it.

No one knows the heartache I carry on. My thoughts are always with you, always a dear memory of the days when you were here.

You want to breathe but can't, the chest pain is unbearable.

It was the spring of 1988, I was 22 years old with a job as a day care worker and living the single life. Lived in a beautiful suburb of Chicago. The lake a few miles away and a children's play park right across the street. It was springtime and all the kids were jumping up and down, laughing and smiling, and waving their hands in the air.

I was enjoying the single life. Free, made my own decisions, wasn't looking when I found love. It took me by surprise; I wasn't looking when he showed up. Something told me we could be friends. We talked, things got serious and before I knew it we were moving in together.

My life was going to change. I was going to have a baby. I knew this life would be a new beginning. A beginning of all things, discovery, hope, and dreams. She was happiness and a blessing.

She discovered her hands and fingers as soon as we brought her home and began sucking on them. Soon she was grasping her rattles and sucking on them as well, she rolled over by herself a couple of weeks later and was walking before she was nine months old. At nine months old she started playing on the bongos. That was her favorite toy. The first year went by so fast. She grew and learned so much; it was hard to keep up with her.

Her grandparents always sang to her and taught her how to do little dances so she recognized music very early. The first song and game she learned was patty cake. Her grandpa taught her how to do the jig. At 4 years old her grandpa taught her the words to "Deep in the Heart of Texas" and they recorded it together, I of course still have a copy but it's very hard to listen to.

For her 1st birthday I bought her a play telephone and a pail and shovel. She loved it. She carried the phone around with her pretending to talk and if I ever noticed something was missing, I learned I had to look in her pail to find it. Her favorite stuffed animals were Bert, Ernie and Big Bird and she always carried her blanket with her.

Lisa was born in April and that meant the weather was soon to get warmer. I was pregnant all winter and now finally could go out and be reminded of all the excitement of spring. I could not wait to introduce Lisa to the swing, bugs, flowers and ice cream. Even going outside after it rained was fun to do, just to splash around a little. While I wanted to take her out in the stroller, Lisa's dad had other ideas. He insisted we stay inside and he go out.

There was a new burst of plant life all around us. It's springtime! Time to go outside and dive in nature. Run through the full green fields, hear the birds sing overhead and smell the fresh flowers in bloom. It was time just to lay in the grass and look up at the airplanes and imagine what shapes the clouds will be. Saving the time and the beauty and putting it in our pocket.

My mom visited soon after Lisa was born so she too could experience this tremendous little joy. She was overjoyed to be with us and to see her first grandchild. I could not wait for my mom to become grandma. She wanted to be a grandma so badly and now finally the time came. Becoming a grandma is an experience that only after becoming a grandma can you begin to appreciate. She wanted to be called Grammie.

She planned on developing what could be the most important relationship in their lives. She planned to love. The best part of being a grandma is that you can love just because they are adorable. There is no such thing as to much love. Grandmothers are an important role in the lives of their granddaughters. This very special and rare relationship can add a special greatness to granddaughter's personality.

She helped me out so much during this time; I could not even express it. She gave Lisa her first bath and took us grocery shopping. Her visit was truly needed, truly a gift. She was so caring and tender. Showing me how to do things, telling me what would be best.

Making memories with someone who will remember them and cherish them for years to come, even after you are long gone. Our family celebrates birthdays and holidays together, with meals, candles, toasts, gifts, lots of laughter and storytelling. My mom is very good at telling stories. She tends to take a long time to tell these stories but I sit and listen because I know I will never get it back.

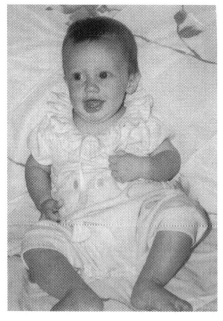

One winter cold day while Lisa was visiting grammie and papa, they spent most of the day making a Mickey Mouse snowman. Papa video taped it and you could tell they all spent many

hours rolling the snow, packing it and adding personal touches. Mickey ears turned out the best. When they were all done they all were taking a breather and looking at their perfect creation when Lisa yelled, "Let's make Minnie"! You could hear my mom sigh out loud. It was very funny.

One other time Lisa was visiting my mom, she and Lisa made cookies. There was flour and sugar all over the kitchen. They decorated the cookies and my mom said she was not sure how much frosting actually made it onto the cookies.

My mom also remembered every time Lisa visited the two of them went shopping and they always bought strawberries. There was not a single time when Lisa was over and there were no strawberries. One weekend Lisa and my mom's parents were visiting. They were all awake very early except for Grammie. Lisa and my grandparents wanted to have strawberries for breakfast . Lisa told great grandma "the strawberries are in the refrigerator" but she could not find them so Lisa stormed into my mom's bedroom with this stern look in her face and a meaningful tone in her voice and said "Grammie you need to come downstairs and find the strawberries for great grandma, she cannot find them." "I tried telling her they are in the refrigerator but she cannot see them." Grammie replied, "Oh Lisa, I am so sorry I don't have any strawberries.

*L*isa's dad and I did not have one of what was a strong foundation to our marriage and to make it worse I was stressed. Worrying about a new baby and her father. My number one priority was to care for Lisa and his was to go out. I was experiencing all the lack of sleepless nights.

I wanted to learn more about being married, but it was just not happening. We never started out with any goals or values so we were not growing or learning. I did not want to ignore the problems because we had Lisa, I did not want anybody to get hurt.

Lisa's dad and I divorced when she was 2 years old. I tried to make the divorce as easy as possible for her. I moved to Wisconsin with Lisa and her dad stayed in Chicago. Visits with her dad were common whether it was her dad coming to our house or Lisa and I going to his house. I went with her on many visits.

I knew by moving away from Lisa's dad's parents, there would be separation from other relatives. Lisa's grandparents were very involved with Lisa and experienced all the happiness and joy of a baby girl. They taught her new songs to sing and dance to and when she first started walking they were there. Seeing her grow and learn was so much fun for them and it had been so long since there was a little girl in the family. Lisa was the first granddaughter so this was so exciting. I knew if I moved away it would crush them but I was not happy where I was.

Going through divorce as a child myself, and did not want to go through it again especially with my own child. I knew about losing contact with relatives. I was uprooted from my perfect little life on a farm with horses, dogs and cats. My cousins were my best friends then and I miss them so much.

When my parents divorced, my dad moved to a suburb of Chicago and my mom, brother and I moved to Wisconsin. So growing up my brother and I traveled to Chicago and the surrounding areas many times. I knew my way around. We visited often and my dad took us to all kinds of events. Baseball games, Taste of Chicago, and museums. When I graduated from high school, I moved to Chicago, first, as a nanny, then as a day care worker.

With my mom's help Lisa and I moved to Wisconsin near my mom and into an apartment building with all others living there who were in a similar situation. Single, with a child, and needing assistance from the state. I learned so much about life at this time. I enrolled in college and was living the life of a single person again.

I was dating but not seriously and met a young man who would later become Lisa's step dad. I was very happy. Happy to be in a safe and secure environment, happy to be taking care of Lisa and happy to be with a new love.

Two years later we were living together and about to welcome a baby. We found out it was a boy. Lisa was excited, so excited she wanted too be the one who named him. We asked her what name she liked and without hesitation she spoke up and said "Jacob. I think you guys will like Jacob", so that's what we named him.

Lisa had a lot going on at this time in her life. She was starting kindergarten and was going to be a big sister. Her step dad and I took these big time events with stride. Although this pregnancy did not go as smooth as my first one, we handled it all together as I was in a much better place to do so.

Jacob was born as an emergency c-section in October 1994. I was in the hospital for 4 nights. Lisa's step dad brought Lisa to visit me and she held Jacob for the very first time. I had what I always wanted a boy and a girl and a loving husband.

About 6 months later, Lisa took Jacob to school and showed him off to her friends. I remembered it was near Lisa's birthday. The teacher took pictures and the children all created a birthday card for her. I read

a story to the kids and Jacob lay on the blanket wide-awake but never cried. Lisa was worried he would cry the whole day and embarrass her but he didn't.

In 2nd grade, Lisa wrote, produced and directed a play. She wrote the script and made enough copies for everyone so everyone in the class had a part, but she needed a baby. After thinking real hard about it, she allowed Jacob to be in it. All he had to do was to sit in a box; he was perfect.

She loved dressing him up in her dolls clothes. One time Lisa took a t-shirt off of one of her dolls and put jeans on Jacob and told him he was Garth Brooks. Jacob ran around the house singing "I'm Grass Rocks". That was as close to saying Garth Brooks as he could get.

When Lisa grew out of her Halloween costumes, she put Jacob in them. One year she dressed him in a wedding dress, which belonged to one of her dolls. She had a wedding dress from earlier so they each had a wedding dress on and played. Two years later, Lisa was Belle and Jacob was a solider. They both were excited about their costumes. They tried them on and when Jacob saw Lisa he said, "you look like a cupcake". After Lisa heard this she went to her room. I thought it was cute and funny and she may have also but just for attention she chose to go to her room.

They played board games together, she watched cartoons with him and taught him how to brush his teeth and make big splashes in the tub then she would dry him off and get his pajamas on. There was always water on the floor but Lisa would tell Jacob not to worry because mom will clean it up.

Jacob was easily amused so Lisa thought of funny, stupid stunts for him to do. She would throw a ball and tell Jacob to go get it and he did, Jacob adored her and always agreed with her.

Lisa went through all the boy crushes girls go through. She liked the Back Street boys and sang their songs quite often around the house. Since Jacob was always interested in doing what Lisa was doing, he wanted to sing too, so Lisa taught him the songs and they both would run around the house singing.

Lisa was fond of dancing and cheer leading. She always would think up cheers but needed a flyer, so she volunteered Jacob. I let her do this once or twice, and then I said no more. I was too afraid someone would get hurt.

Lisa and Jacob both love to show off and perform. They both enjoy acting. Lisa always tried out for one of the leads in all the school musicals, although she never got a lead, she always had a dance solo or a few lines.

Jacob loves to be the comedian and a magician. He likes to tell jokes, tell the punch line, and hear the laughter. Jacob takes humor and magic seriously. They both used the power of thought and imagination to overcome the feeling of stage freight.

Lisa was a fan of Lucille Ball, Shirley Temple, Mary Kate and Ashley Olsen, Grease, The Sound Of Music and The Wizard Of OZ. All the music and dancing, what talent they all had. Lisa had all the vhs tapes of the Olsen twins and anytime there was a new one that came out, her dad would get it for her. Jacob started watching them with her and again they both sang and danced around.

Lisa and I lived in Wisconsin and her dad lived in Chicago, she made several trips to Chicago. She loved the big city; she was Chicago's biggest fan. Wrigley field and the Cubs were her favorite. Pizza places, Navy Pier and the zoo, were all big hot spots for her and her dad. The lake was awesome, so pretty and the views especially at night brought magic and glitter. She loved to tell people she was born in Chicago. It was a thrill for her; it brought more attention to her.

I had developed an addiction to the Cubbies and Lisa saw this in me. I have some awesome memories of Wrigley Field. The first baseball game I ever went to was the Pirates and the Cubs, the Cubs won. The behaviors of the players was fun to watch, I never expected them to be perfect but it was just plain fun to be a part of the cheers and originality of the park. I liked Harry Carey, as funny stupid as it was I liked him. Lisa's very first baseball game was at Wrigley Field she was 3 years old. Whenever she came home from visiting her dad, she had a new Cubs shirt or souvenir of some sort.

Lisa's Aunt wrote an awesome description of Lisa and the times she got to spend with her.

> *My niece Lisa always brought so much joy to the family. Although she lived a few hours away in Wisconsin, we got to see her often on her visits to be with her Chicago family. As well as I thought I knew my niece, it wasn't until she was taken from us that I found out much of her personality.*
>
> *As a small child it was obvious Lisa was creative and imaginative.*
>
> *She loved dolls, music and movies. When she would come to my house she would enjoy playing dress-up and exploring my jewelry box.*

She would tell me she loved coming to my house because there was so much to look at.

From a young age she was fascinated with my black satin toe shoes, which I kept on a doorknob, a memory or my own childhood as a dancer.

We knew she loved to move and dance. I can recall her as a four year old wiggling around to the Spice Girls. She had a real appreciation for all the arts and her father, my brother, would take her to music stores, concerts and ice-skating shows. Grandma would take her shopping in the big Chi town stores she was a small town girl with a big city heart.

Lisa's parents encouraged her interest in the arts by providing her with classes in dance and gymnastics. She was " a natural" and eventually became an accomplished cheerleader... Lisa was the girl at the top of the pyramid, unafraid to be lifted and thrown, thrilled to fly through the air, always trusting her own abilities and that her team-mates would be there to catch her every time.

As Lisa made her way through high school she added plays and choir concerts to her busy cheerleading schedule. But she was a teenager who always had a concern for the needs and care of others. It was not surprising when she chose nursing as her college major.

Lisa standing outside Navy Pier

It wasn't until after her death that we heard from a pastor that Lisa had started a food pantry for the needy in her town, and although it wasn't even at her own church, she would continue to volunteer there on her visits home during college breaks.

I wanted to support her interest in dance so I invited her to accompany me to one of my movement classes when she was in town for a few days. After the class we stopped at Starbucks and Lisa told me it the very first time she had been there.

It was the first of many Starbucks sweet treats to come, but not nearly as many as I had hoped. I wish we could go there together again… how could we know how short her future would be?

She was maturing into a delightful young woman, but we really had no idea how much motivation and leadership she was showing at school. Yes, we knew she had been chosen as an R.A. on her dormitory floor, but what we came to find was that when Lisa arrived at the University of Dubuque and found that there was no dance team – she decided to start one! The dance troupe continues today in her honor.

Some of her accomplishments were revealed to us at her memorial service and some things were uncovered in the sad days before.

It's not surprising that a student nurse would be registered to be an organ donor, but we soon learned that when Lisa shared this wish with her mother she also made the request to be buried with her Grandpa in Chicago, should anything happen to her…

Lisa was always a joy to us in life and she continues to be an inspiration, even though her life here on earth with us has ended.

Lisa's Uncle Tim Wrote:

She certainly soared while she was with us. I'm sure she is still soaring! Lisa brought so much happiness into the world. I miss her dearly, but can't help but smile when I think of all the funny things see did when visiting. Love to you and the family.

*L*isa wanted a puppy so as a confirmation gift her step dad and I bought her one. Lisa had always been interested in training and socializing a puppy that would be later used in helping the blind. Since it was taking a long time to get information sent to us, she decided in helping a puppy who needed a home and who would otherwise be uthinized. So before I knew it, a little tiny puppy was delivered to our home.

Lisa was a mama and she loved it. The nights were rough in the beginning but soon Lisa had the puppy sleeping with her in her bed. Of course Lisa named the puppy Lucy. Lucy was so excited when Lisa came home from school; they were the best of friends.

Lucy followed Lisa everywhere, now she follows me. She keeps me in sight even when I use the bathroom she lays in front of the door. If I move into a different room, she follows. I am grateful we adopted Lucy, she comforted Lisa, and now she comforts me. Lucy spends a lot of time outside chasing lizards and I am sure Lisa is laughing at how funny it is to watch.

Lisa holding her puppy

When Lisa was 15 years old, she talked to me about donating organs. She signed the back of her driver's license and verbally told me what her wishes were. When she was old enough she donated blood. She knew how important donating blood was to someone who needed it. She bribed her friends telling them, "If you come with me and donate blood I will buy you a sub". She always read stories of people donating organs, and those who still were in need.

She always considered herself a perfect organ donor. Since the opportunity to donate an organ had not come, she donated blood. The thought of donating blood saved three people's lives every time she did it, made her feel needed and again brought attention onto herself. She loved being the hero.

I hoped we would never need to make the decision to donate one of our families' organs but I knew it could happen. I knew the thought of having to make a decision about donating a loved one's organs could happen because of my nephew Eric. Eric didn't need an organ, he needed a bone marrow transplant. Lisa wanted to be tested to find out if she could be the donor but the doctors started out with the siblings first.

It began 6/8/2003 - Eric's dad sent an email to all friends and relatives trying to explain some very bad and unfortunate news on their son. "Our son Eric has leukemia. He didn't have any symptoms until a few weeks ago when his teeth were bothering him. A visit to the dentist confirmed impacted wisdom teeth. All four teeth were removed. Following the procedure, Eric had a range of problems, mainly fevers and dehydration. A blood test at the hospital confirmed leukemia."

Eric's bone marrow biopsy determined that the type of leukemia he has is acute myelogenous leukemia. Eric started chemo follow-up treatments and could have a bone marrow transplant. His siblings, Steve, Lindsey and Mike will have their blood drawn. A few weeks later, it was confirmed that Eric's older brother Mike is the match and will be the donor for an Allogeneic Stem Cell Transplant.

The challenge was for Eric's body to accept Mike's donation as his own. Eventually Eric will have Mike's blood type and immune system. Mike's bone marrow started fighting and Eric was in remission.

October 21 2004 Started the first year of celebrations for Eric. He was in remission. This celebration would last four years. In 2007 Eric relapses. The doctors find out that Mike's bone marrow is too close of a match for Eric so they go to his second match, his sister for help.

April 2008 Eric received a stem cell transplant from his younger sister Lindsey but then on August 5th he relapsed again.

Summer of 2009 Eric put together a bucket list of things he wanted to do with the time he had left. In June 2009, he went on a skydiving adventure.

June 14th 2009, Eric threw out the first pitch at a Brewer game. Other things included taking trips, one to Las Vegas and also to New York.

August 13th 2009 Eric is given Decitabine/Mylotarg. The Decitabine/Mylotarg treatment is working as the cancer cells have been reduced by half! A month later, initial tests show that bone marrow is still clear of any obvious leukemia.

January 1st 2011, Bone marrow biopsy results are positive. Eric's leukemia has returned.

July 27th 2011 Eric relapses to fight AML for the 5th time and is admitted inpatient to Froedtert. July 30th 2011 6 day regimen begins of a Ara-C and Cladrabine cocktail ("Clag") and neupogen. The neupogen is meant to spur rapid growth of the white blood cells, it helps the chemotherapy identify and kills them.

August 10th 2011- Eric has high fevers and his white blood cell counts are not functioning well.

August 16th 2011– Eric and his wife celebrate one month of being married. Eric achieves remission status for the 5th time after just 1 chemotherapy treatment!

September 11th 2011– Eric's doctors have found 2 bone marrow donors who are not related to the family.

September 24th 2011- Eric is in the hospital getting the 3rd out of 5 CLAG Chemo regimen, which is an insurance policyto keep the leukemia away while we continue to prepare for the big stem cell transplant.

October 18th 2011 - Long day at Froedtert … labs, bone marrow biopsy, MUGA, CT scan, bone density scans, pulmonary function tests… all to make sure his body is ready for the stem cell transplant in a few weeks.

October 24th 2011 – Eric and Mike met with Dr. James Shull and Dr. Jing Zhang of the McArdle Laboratory for Cancer Research and donated $10,000 towards leukemia research study on behalf of L.I.F.E. Then they went on a tour of the building and got a glimpse of what happens behind the scenes.

Eric just wants his long battle with cancer to be over with. "A year from now, I'd like to be working, shoveling snow, mowing the lawn, cooking dinner and just relaxing watching a movie."

It has been estimated Eric's odds are slightly in his favor that he will survive the transplant, and it remains his only current option for a cure. Eric's donor was determined to have a tissue (HLA) type that matches. Matching is performed on the basis of variability at three or more loci of the HLA gene, and a perfect match at these loci is preferred.

Eric's previous two donors were his brother Mike and sister Lindsey but after 4 and 1 years respectively post transplant, both proved unsuccessful. After 3 more relapses, it was decided to pursue a 3rd unrelated donor which has now been found in Europe through a registry. After the cells are harvested from the donor, they will be transported to the hospital where Eric will receive them through an intravenous line just like a blood transfusion, and will take approximately 4-5 hours to complete. Following the transplant, Eric will need to be kept in a quarantined environment and need to receive periodic transfusions of red cells and platelets until his marrow function has been restored by the transplanted stem cells.

Dancing, music, singing and cheer leading was a huge part of Lisa's life. I noticed her grow and mature as a leader. An important trait of any squad member is to be a person of good character. Emotions can run high whether it be preparing for a competition or cheering on your football team and fans; a cheerleader must be energetic, optimistic, and composed. As the anticipation increases, teams must continue to encourage one another in order to achieve the shared goal of a win.

Cheerleaders develop friendships that will often last a lifetime. The team grows and matures, developing life skills that will benefit the cheerleader forever. The sport of cheer leading teaches hard work, perseverance, competitiveness, and teamwork. The qualities of a cheerleader, friendliness, respectfulness, and accountability are all skills that will benefit in the future. All activities that helped with children, disabled adults, the elderly and those in emergency need Lisa was all for it, going forward and wanting to do bigger and better things. She wanted to go further and always thinking of ways to exceed.

Not only did Lisa actively participate in cheer leading in high school but also she took all that enthusiasm to the other parts of her life.

Lisa's High School Cheer leading Renee Pastorius wrote:

The Marshmallow Prank

It happened one Thursday night, after a wrestling meet, in 2007.Phone rings at about 11:30p.m., I pick up the phone and in an already sleeping voice say, "hello?" "Hi, Coach? We are in trouble and I don't know what to do!", the voice on the other end of the phone replies. To hearing this, I am now sitting straight up in bed, eyes completely open, and realizing it's Lisa on the other end of the phone."Oh my god, are you O.k.? Is everyone alright? (tone changing to harsher scolding tone) Where are you? Do I have to come get you?", now my husband is sitting up in bed and looking at me with worry."No, NO, NO! It's nothing like that!", she informs me."Then what in the world did you do?" I asked

"Well, we came up to town to Taco Bell and saw that the wrestlers were all inside, so we decided to marshmallow their cars and now they are mad at us. They said they are going to go to all of our houses and break things and wreck things! And I don't know what to do!" Lisa says frantically.My reply, " WHAT? YOU WHAT?" "Marsh mellowed their cars," Lisa replies again. "What the Hell is Marshmallowing someone's car?", to my dismay. Her reply, " you know, you get marshmallows and bite them in half, then stick them on the windows of cars, in

14

the winter, because then they freeze on the window, and you can't use the windshield wipers, because they just will hit the marshmallows. It looks like the car is full of zits!"

I burst out laughing at the silliness of this and then scolded her for waking me up with this kind of goofiness and scaring me half to death. But she wasn't really happy with my reaction. So, the story goes, they marsh mellowed the boys cars when they were inside eating. Some other girls saw them doing it and told the boys who did it and all. The boys then started to call the wrestling cheerleaders and told them, they were in big trouble and if they didn't fess up to it, they were going to go to all the girls houses and do something to whatever car was outside.

The girls were freaking out, because most of the cars at home were the parents cars! To this I replied, " Well, you did it, call them up and tell them you all did it." Lisa said, " No, we already denied it!"

We can't go back and take it all back, it would make us look stupid!" I told her it wouldn't make you look stupid, it will make them fess up and do the right thing. They were already caught, and now call them. "Call them up, tell them you all did it, but you didn't do it to get them mad. So, say your sorry and that you will meet them at the closest gas station. That way you all can use the window cleaner and help get the marshmallows off. Maybe if you all help get them off the window, it may just end up being a fun night!" I told Lisa. She thought this was a good idea, although reluctant and did it anyways.

That following Monday, at practice, I found out she did exactly what I said. They met up with the boys, helped them clean it up, and then they all ended up going over to someone's house and hung out. They all had a good time, nothing was broke, wrecked, and no one was really mad at the prank! The rest of the year, was filled with pranks going back and forth! I will never forget that phone call and I have to admit, I have gone Marshmallowing since!!! Thanks Lisa for teaching her Coach a new trick!!

In 2005 Lisa competed for the crown in the Theresa Firefighter's Queen competition and won. The day of the interview, I dropped her off at the fire station and an hour later; she exited with a crown on her head, a big bouquet of roses and a banner across the front of her displaying the title of Theresa Firefighter Queen. She wanted me to take her home so we could take pictures, then she had to go to all her friends houses without telling them, enter their house and surprise them.

She was in all the little town parades every weekend and newspapers from all over would come and take pictures, she loved all that attention.

Pictures in the paper, me taking pictures for our album, her friends watching her ride down the street on a big float or on a fire truck, the sirens blaring and the dresses and tiaras she wore all such a joy for her, smiling and waving the whole time.

She participated in all the local town's firefighter's annual picnics and wore her banner and tiara. Then a few weeks before the final parade of the summer, she was to compete at the Dodge County Firefighters Queen Tournament, and she won that as well. In the final parade of the summer, she rode as Dodge Firefighter Queen and Theresa Firefighter Queen on a big float, with her court. Her court included Firefighter Queens from local towns all in Dodge County.

The following year she crowned the new Theresa Firefighter Queen and the new Dodge County Firefighter Queen. She also was a judge in the Dodge County Queen Tournament.

My daughter maintained her independence. She had the normal teenage girl attitude, know it all, desire to prove she can do anything and expression of a strong view of her own. The most common issues we may have fought about were fashion, appearances, and attitude. I reacted with frustration instead of an understanding. I focused all my attention on her outer most feelings and not paying attention to her inner most feelings. She stood up for herself. She was passionate about her feelings and demanded to be treated fairly.

Lisa's Essay on High School, What she learned, and her Future:

I've grown up so much since starting high school. As a freshman, you are nervous and somewhat unaware of your surroundings. Trying to figure out what's what and to fit in. That definitely describes me my first year.

I joined football and basketball cheer leading, International Club, musicals and choir, all just for fun, that year I learned a new phrase called "Time Management".

It took quite a while to figure out how to make time to be in fun activities, study, hand in all my homework on time, and get the occasional 6 hours of sleep.

The faculty and coaches were all very helpful to me along the way. Teachers were understanding and made sure to fit in time during their busy schedules to help answer my questions.

By the middle of the year, managing my time successfully became easier and helped my life run smoother. Since then, I've carried that skill with me. Almost every semester since then, there has been no room for study halls.

Managing my schedule of activities and grades got even harder. I've learned to take a lot of responsibility for what I do. I think that I'm mature enough now to make responsible decisions on what activities or clubs to be in, this left no excuses for getting behind or failing classes. Unfortunately, not as many students as should have took the initiative to keep up their grades. I'm more reassured knowing that since I became comfortable asking for help in high school classes, seeking help in my college classes will be easy.

Besides just becoming more mature and responsible, my education here at Lomira has brought me to be a better-rounded individual in general.

I've learned to take classes based on what I need for my future, not just what my friends are taking, to manage my time and make sure that my grades are what they need to be, and how to be a well functioning member of society.

Michelle Schwanz wrote:

I remember the first time we met, you were in 3rd grade. I directed you to play Vincent Van Gogh. I still chuckle at the memories of the gigantic bandage that covered your ear! Good-old Vincent never looked so beautiful! Will you ever forgive me for thrusting you into that demanding role? A rising star was born! Your sparkle will be sadly missed, as well as your gorgeous baby-blues. They were the windows to your beautiful soul… You added a loving dimension to our school, community, and to our family. I'll miss our talks, your smile, and your laughter. Most of all, I'll miss the happiness you brought into our home. You were a loyal and loving friend to Lauren. Watching you two silly gals feed off of each other's energy was an exciting sight to behold. Never a dull moment around those awesome LHS Wrestling Cheerleaders. You girls have an indelible bond of friendship. I can see that your shared experiences shaped and enriched each other's lives. Isn't great to know that you are tucked safely into one another's hearts? Thanks for leading us to a better way… on EARTH… as well as HEAVEN. We love you sweet Lisa, you will remain in our hearts and memories forever.

Lisa had such good grades in high school; she was able to take advantage of a program called school to work. It was a program that uses the classroom and the community to help students with hands on learning. She decided without any doubt to take up nursing. Lisa had desire to be a public servant, lots of dedication, positive attitude, and enthusiasm.

She was in high school and a nursing student. Everybody at the hospital loved her and knew she was going to make a difference in the nursing field. She did make a difference. She felt it. I felt it.

Having the capabilities to say hello to strangers is such an incredible ability. One of the most giving gestures we can do, to open ourselves just as we are, in a short amount of time, to make a connection and to continue the circle of life.

Lisa knew walking through the hospital doors would spark a lot of questions and thoughts of what lie ahead. She held her head up, and walked in with pride. She needed to hold their hand and comfort them.

When my grandpa died, we all knew it was coming. His body showed the last stages of life. The hospice nurse told us that's normal and there's nothing we could do. My grandpa did not want to be in the hospital waiting to die so there was a bed made for him in the living room.

My grandma of took care of him and waited on him. She would spend 20 hours a day taking care of him by herself.

The last four days of his life, she became so exhausted. I received a phone call from her telling me how grandpa was in need of being picked up and carried, she tried to do it but couldn't. Hearing this I cried. I collected my thoughts, packed a few things and drove to be with them and to take care of what I could. Lisa wanted to go with, knowing she was mature enough and emotionally able, I asked but my grandma thought it best she stay at home until further notice.

I was not expecting to see my grandpa awake. The hospice nurse and my grandma were sitting with my grandpa when we walked in. My grandpa and said "Hi Aim".

Those words were golden. The hospice nurse's mouth fell open and he said "wow, those words need to stay with you forever, as they may be the last".

A couple of hours later my mom arrived at the house. We all had the same thoughts, hopes and reality.

The night before he died, I rested on the couch while grandma got to sleep upstairs in her own bed.

There were specific instructions on what to do if grandpa stopped breathing, it not include CPR. He did not want to be resuscitated and signed papers for us not to do so.

I listened to him breathe for fear it would be his last, then for several seconds, so I thought this is it, this is his last breath, then he would breathe.

There were two seconds of intermission for every 1 breath. This is normal. His mouth was open and we could hear what sounded like congestion in his chest. We held his hands and told him it was okay to go and we'd take care of grandma. I think that was what he needed to hear because he passed away shortly after.

I had never seen anybody die before. I am so glad we were there. My mom, grandma and I as we stood there near my grandpa's bed holding his hand, I thought of so many memories.

My memories were different from my mom's or my grandma's but we all had precious time with him and enjoyed it so very much.

Each room in that house held it's own memory. Christmas, Thanksgiving, and Easter dinners. All of us gathered, all of us together, with all the smells and lights filling the air. Nothing could be better.

Grandpa loved to show movies on his reel-to-reel projector. They had quite the collection. The fat guy and the skinny guy (Laurel and Hardy) and the funny man. They also had movies of my brother and I when we were kids and movies of their own kids. All of them silent of course but all brought such joy to us each time we saw them. How I would love to see them again, hopefully I will soon.

I remembered how my grandpa loved to eat lunch on the patio, the beautiful patio with all the blooming flowers. My grandma always had such beautiful flowers, all of which she remembered exactly where each flower came from.

I remembered while sitting on the patio, the jets that flew over and the noise they made. To this day, whenever I am outside and jets fly overhead, I close my eyes and relax and remember the good times we had on my grandparent's patio. I will always have this memory.

Grandma and Grandpa's patio

Lisa found the positive side in everything, knew what to say to patients, praise them and encouraged them in every way. If patients were uneasy, her soft sweet voice would quiet them. She never had a problem with words; and it never took her long to warm up. She had been instructed to not delay to do the work that needs to be done. The time is now; we have no time to lose. She is to look work right in the face and advance as fast as possible. She answered his call knowing others are waiting for this burden to be removed. She was a companion on the journey.

Lisa loved sunrises. She greeted every day. Every morning she always took a moment to take a long look out her windows, pull back the curtains, greet the sunrise and just be grateful for another day. She was always focused on her objectives for the day. She trusted her inner strength to solve any problem. Smiled and was cheerful.

Hugs, hugs, hugs, that was simple and an easy way to show someone how much she cared about them. Sometimes a friendly hug can brighten someone's day, and it's a fun and easy way to help make the world a brighter place.

Her greatest power was the power to choose how to express herself. She knew the reality is what brought her to the present moment, the now. Whatever great opportunities she missed in the past were not as important as the opportunities that lie ahead. She comforted patients and told them that they shouldn't be sad.

Lisa had a big heart, believed in herself and took time to enjoy her friends and family and all her surroundings. She followed her heart. Constantly working towards her goals and helped so much with others reaching their goals. Lived life to the fullest and believed in tomorrow.

Lisa made things happen; she did not just sit and wait for it. If it wasn't there in front of her, she went out to get it. If someone would have told her "no it's not possible" she looked at it as their weakness, she worked to help that person with their weakness and then moved on. She taught strength and persistence.

In 2008, while Lisa was working her shift at the hospital, she met Eric. Eric was a firefighter/EMT and they saw a lot of each other at the hospital. One evening after their shift they went out and talked. They talked till 5 in the morning. She found someone who was her equal, who shared her same love of life and like her wanted to dedicate his life to helping others. Lisa told me" I've never met someone I have so much in common with," The two fell head over heels in love. On the weekends they would take turns,

Eric going to Iowa for a weekend, and Lisa coming back here, to be with Eric, his family and friends, and her family and friends.

Eric had already had the experience of helping to deliver a baby. Eric and the other team members received a 911 call. They heard a lady was having a baby and needed a ride to the hospital. When Eric and the team got there, the baby was crowning, so Eric did what he could with helping to ease the baby out.

Kirby wrote:

> *One of my favorite memories with Lisa was when her grammie came to town. Lisa was so very excited for her to come visit; she had to have the best for her grammie. She had to see the hotel room before she got it; she had shrimp and a jacuzzi especially for her. She was so excited she planned the weekend so that all of her bestest friends got to meet her. So, I went over with some other friends, played the Newlywed game; which Lisa and Adam won! We made time to go swimming and just relax. I think Lisa wore her grandma out a little but they were both nothing but smiles the entire time.*
>
> *I never got the chance to meet Eric, but Lisa was so in love and couldn't wait for me to do so. One afternoon as we sat in the UPC office she proceeded to tell me more about him and all that they had done all summer and how it was no fun to leave him every weekend. Then of course, as we continue our girl talk, her cell phone rang, it was Eric, so they chat for a bit and she blushes and shines as they talk. After their conversation she continues to tell me more about him. She mentioned something in our conversation that felt like nothing that day, however less than a month later it hit like a tornado. She told me that she prayed he would not die before her, something she thought about because he was a firefighter, because she couldn't imagine life without him. Every time I think about this conversation I break into tears. The simplest girl talk conversation held more than I could have ever imagined. Well Lisa, you left all of us far too early, but we are now all blessed with one of the greatest angels ever.*

Lisa knew the strength and courage of a firefighter. They lay their lives on the line in the most uncertain and dangerous circumstances. She knew she would spend night after night wondering and waiting to hear from him, hoping with faith that he makes it safely back into her arms.

Lisa had many really close friends in high school. She shared thoughts, stories, emotions, homework, and boyfriends. They continued this ritual up until their senior year. They were a circle of best friends who had a good time together.

Friends are a great way to have fun, make new friends, learn about yourself, and open the door to possible future careers. Spending time together and working for a familiar goal, they have the chance to form lasting friendships. Friends in many cases become like family helping you to deal with life's little bumps and turns.

This was a connection her group of friends shared that other people couldn't experience. As a teenager myself, I never even had this kind of connection with my friends the way Lisa and her friends had it so I didn't understand. With so many friends, there was a lot going on. So many stories and rumors. So many attitudes.

Stephanie wrote:

> On the last day of lion select, Lisa and I and the whole rest of the choir went to McDonald's. We all got caught when we got back. Everyone got detention except Lisa and I who got to clean the costume room … chasing a state owned vehicle down highway 41 because Lisa and I were convinced Prince William was in the back seat. Spending countless hours rehearsing for the musicals. Spending free periods in the nurses office visiting or decorating. Our trip to new York when we had piggy back races through grand central station. Lisa's shorts that are still at the bottom of the Pastorius' pond. If they are ever found they will be framed and hung by the pond. I could go on and on with years of side-by-side memories. Her memory lives on in the hearts of many. She impacted so many lives with her kindness and generosity. I hope all is going well with you and the family.

Kelsey Wrote:

> Here's my memory and feelings about Lisa-I remember talking ALL the time with Lisa while we were together, there was never a dull moment. We would talk about boys, and our parents, friends and our funny grandparents, school and siblings.
> I remember one time we talked about our grandparents and she had told me that her grammie flies in her dreams. For quite a few days

after that I remember we would talk to each other in the morning to see if one of us conquered it haha.

While we were in school we used to switch homework to write each other's answers because neither of us liked our own handwriting, but wanted the others.

Lisa was my first "legit" friend when I came into the Lomira Public Schools... sure I knew other people from sports and what not, but none of them befriended me like Lisa did. I sometimes wonder where we would get the crazy ideas we did though, like trying to pull off that we were twins at a Ponderosa while wearing what looked like homecoming dresses. Or staying up 'til dumb hours of the night and trying to make a pizza quietly as to not awake her mom (our mom by this time).

I remember one of her birthdays there were a bunch of girls over and we had some delicious ice cream cake. After we sang happy birthday to her, two girls and I whispered to one another and shoved her face into the cake. I'm sure it was really cold and probably didn't feel the best since it was frozen, but we all laughed regardless.

Lisa always brought out the best in people and was able to see the good in them, its a trait not many acquire over years of life. Many love her, and I'm sure she is up in heaven having the time of her life watching us all down here. We love you Lisa.

In 2007, Lisa attended the University of Dubuque. She chose the University because it has an excellent nursing program with brand-new facilities and most of all, because people come first at the University. She fit right in with many other students and faculty who are the pride of the Midwest and the whole world.

Her roommate in college was another one of her very best friends. Kellie. Kellie was in the nursing program as well. Meeting Lisa and becoming her best friend was the best thing that ever happened to her. A year and a half went by, they could not be separated. A new year of college classes and experiences was about to start and Kellie and Lisa were still going strong, still wanting to do the best that they could and take on so much more. They worked together so strong.

Kellie remembered when Lisa wanted to sign up for an elective class called "Broadway". Kellie said "fine you do that". Lisa asked Kellie to sign up and go with her, the class was at 7:00am, Kellie said "no it's too early, I want to sleep". Lisa begged and begged, finally Kellie said she would. Kellie said it was so much fun she really was glad she joined her.

Kellie's whole world changed overnight, her whole college success and dreams were crushed. Kellie could not think about school. She sat right next to Lisa in all of their classes, she would look over to her side and see an empty seat, and burst out crying and have to leave the room.

Side by side they were one. Kellie and Lisa knew how to do this because they had each other. With so many nursing classes and practices and on the job training, nursing was a difficult program to study for. Kellie could get through it because Lisa was helping, and Lisa could get through it because she had Kellie.

Lisa and Kellie

Kellie remembered a strange but wonderful event just a few days after Lisa's death. She remembered having to go to the library to do some homework. "It was 6 am, very early, I couldn't sleep and knew I had some work that was several days late. I sat at the computer waiting for it to turn on, while I was waiting I heard what sounded like someone typing on a keyboard.

I looked around, I heard it again, I looked around again, I noticed a message on my computer screen. It read "what are you looking for?" My eyes teared up, I tried to speak, I said what? Who's there? Is this you? Lisa? I never got a reply back and always wonder but I think it was her."

"It was just so odd because nobody knew I left to go to the library, it was so early, I didn't want to wake anyone. I wasn't on any kind of a chat online, just Microsoft word, had checked my emails but did not compose any message, just checked them, then this message appeared."

Since some of her friends wrote a memory of the time they had with her in Dubuque, I thought I would write a very special memory I had when I went to visit her:

I drove to Dubuque when Lisa was in her first year. The ride wasn't too long and was very pretty. When I got there, she gave me the grand tour. She showed me her dorm room, the kitchen, and where the boys resided. There was also the laundry room in which she pointed out that quarters from home would come in quite handy. We rented a hotel room near the college. Later we went out to eat, we talked, and we just spent time walking. The next day very early, we went out for breakfast. Then we went horseback riding. Lisa was a member of the recreational staff at Dubuque and what they did was they scheduled several trips and events for the college students to sign up for and participate in.

That particular weekend they scheduled horseback riding at a nearby stable; there was a fair amount of people who took part. It was a lot of fun.

One weekend Lisa and some friends went bowling. She was excited because Adam was also going bowling with them and she wanted to get to know him better. Everybody was enjoying their time and everything was going the way she wanted it to. We received a phone call at about 1 or 2 am from the hospital telling us Lisa was in a bowling accident. Apparently Adam thought it would be a good idea to pick up a bowling ball and throw it at exactly the same time as Lisa threw hers.

The two bowling balls collided and Lisa hadn't let go of her bowling ball, Lisa's finger was in between. Her finger broke; she needed an ambulance ride, x-rays and stitches. There were pictures in the hospital of Adam crying, one close up of her finger and one of Adam and Lisa smiling while she lie in the bed all wrapped up. She was given a prescription for the pain, and there was a lot of it.

She was being such a good sport about it but really her finger hurt so badly and she said the pain pills were only causing her to miss classes because they made her sleepy. Adam and all her friends helped her to carry her books, take notes and even write her papers.

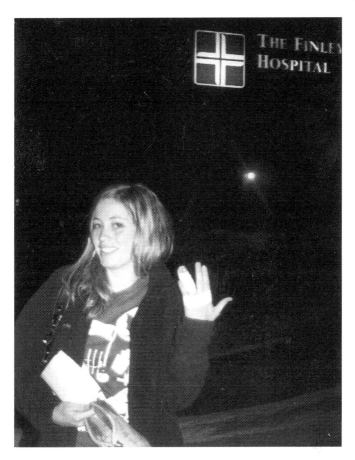

Amanda wrote:

Lisa and I were both in Sociology together, and we both happened to have a problem with putting our phones down and studying. We were doing one of our studying nights late on Monday and she shouts out of nowhere "Oh no I forgot my fish in my car!" We run downstairs to her car, just to find her fish floating upside down. Not only had Lisa left them in a tupper ware container with NO holes, but she also left them in the car when the temperature had been in the triple digits. Lisa started laughing and told me it wasn't even Friday, because we were pretty sure that we had cooked the fish in her car. She then looked at me and told me that the one on top was Waldo. We took the fish upstairs and gave them a proper flushing. Later that week we went to the store together and bought her a new Beta and a little fish bowl and everything. We picked out the fish that did not look the best because we thought no one else would want it, so we wanted to give it a good home. I can remember us trying to get it to follow our finger when we moved it across the bowl.

I can remember she and I playing Pretty Pretty Princess together, and she of course liked to always get the crown. I'll never forget the time I actually won the crown though.

The most important thing of all, I can remember the last thing she ever said to me was, "Don't worry, I promise I will never leave you." I know that Lisa would never break a promise, and I know that she will always be there for me. I had been going through a really rough time that week because a friend of mine had passed away and I had just gotten back from his funeral. I told Lisa that I did not want any more friends because I could not stand the thought of losing another friend. Lisa then took her hand and put it on my chin and told me should would never leave me. Lisa is the most amazing person I have ever met in my life, and I am so lucky to have her as my best friend. I know that she is always by my side.

Stacey wrote:

Lisa and I met our freshman year of college at the University of Dubuque. We were both interested in cheerleading and dance, which began our friendship within the first few days of school. Our freshman year we both were involved in the cheer squad but there was something missing from the experience. Lisa then took it upon herself to contact an instructor and form the University of Dubuque Dance Team named the Spartanettes. At the beginning of the fall semester of our sophomore year Lisa told me about all her hard work she had done to get this group going and how excited she was about it. She asked me probably every day if I would be a part of the group and I told her not to worry that I would be at the meeting and would help her out with anything. At our first group meeting we had quite a few girls interested, which made Lisa ecstatic. Not long after we began practicing at six in the morning for a couple hours. Lisa and I drove together most mornings and even at that early hour she was always excited about a new idea she had for a routine and was pumped to start stretching and dancing. My last memory of her was getting out of her car after dance and just saying "See you later" like every other morning. I could have never imagined we wouldn't be doing that ever again. Going to dance every morning after that was never the same. We all knew Lisa was the one with the dream for this group and there was no way we were letting her dream go. We continued to practice and preformed our first routine at a football game on a beautiful clear day. We brought her uniform to the sideline with us and we danced our hearts out for that girl. Even though she never got to wear that uniform or dance with us on that football field her dream of creating a dance team at the University of Dubuque came true and changed many lives.

One of my best memories of Lisa is from my 19th Birthday during our freshman year of college at the University of Dubuque. It was my golden birthday and Lisa was always adamant about making everyone's birthdays the best they could be and mine was no exception. It was raining that April day but that wasn't going to stop anyone from having a good time and celebrating. I came back to the dorms that afternoon to my room decorated with balloons, streamers, and signs from my friends. That evening after countless outfit changes and pictures together all of us went out to eat supper where I was showered with cards and fun gifts from everyone.

Lisa always made gifts personal and made sure she found my favorite juice drink I drank all the time and tied a balloon to it. After that we went bowling and Lisa added her special touch by requesting my favorite song to be played while we were bowling. After a night of fun I came back to my room to find cake and ice cream. My first birthday away from home was one of my best thanks to all my friends. Lisa and the girls from 2nd floor A-town became like family in the short time we lived together. There are so many unforgettable moments we shared it is hard to explain except that I wouldn't trade any of it for the world.

Krystle Feehan wrote:

The first time I met Lisa was at UD in our dorm building she was always so friendly and introduced herself to myself and my roommate. Every time I think of Lisa I think of her beautiful smile. I do not think I ever saw her without a smile on her face. She was always so friendly to everyone! Lisa was an amazing person and now she is an even more amazing angel watching over us all. I know she has been watching over us the past few years and making sure all has been good. The day my son was born was the third year anniversary of Lisa's death and I knew she was there watching over us and I will forever remember her on that day.

*I*t *was late at night* when we received the phone call every parent hates to get. It was from the Dubuque police telling us there was an accident and our daughter was hurt. All I heard was "gosh, this isn't good, I hate to have to tell you this, oh this doesn't look good; your daughter was in a motorcycle accident." The police office continued, "There was no blood pressure, no pulse, and CPR was administered." In response I stuttered with my words, "what?" "who is this?" "this can't be right" "I am sorry you must have the wrong number" "are you sure?" "Lisa wouldn't have been on a motorcycle, she doesn't have a motorcycle" "How do you know this is my daughter Lisa?"

According to the Dubuque Police Department, the driver of the motorcycle was traveling southbound in the northbound lanes of Kerper Blvd around 9:00 pm. on Wednesday night. Police say Chase hit a northbound vehicle near the intersection of Kerper Blvd. and Fengler Street. Lisa was the passenger on the motorcycle. Martin was taken to Finley Hospital in Dubuque and then flown to the University of Iowa Hospitals and Clinics. Both were students of the University of Dubuque.

The officer was talking so fast and with so much fear. I could hear people moving and running around. If that was not bad enough, the police officer told me CPR was administered; there was no pulse and no blood pressure. I was numb hearing this, I didn't know what to say, I didn't know what to do. I was told she had to have a quick scan done on her head, and then the doctors would call us back to let us know what they would have to do. The doctors soon called back and told us they had to transport her on flight for life to another hospital, the best hospital in Iowa, University of Iowa.

We arrived at the hospital at 5:00am and were rushed into one of those "family rooms" where they give you bad news. I will never forget the words, the emotions, and the concerns of the doctors and the counselors. One look at them and I could feel the pain in my chest going deeper and more painful.

I knew it wasn't good, I couldn't breathe, I couldn't think. I kept feeling this pain in my heart and in my neck.

This was still not real. Anger raced in my head. Doctors just looked at me with no expression and with sad eyes. After several minutes of trying to listen to the doctors explain procedures, I asked, "You mean she's never going to wake up"? The doctor looked at me with his head down, and said,

"A neurologist will have to come in to examine her." The doctor said, he could not even talk and when he did, he spoke so quietly. It was as if he was mourning.

We finally were able to see her. She didn't look good. It was so sad. No one could have prepared me for the feelings that came over me when I saw my daughter with all those injuries. What a nightmare, how could this be happening? I was sure they had the wrong person; they must have brought me to the wrong bed. I asked "so when is she going to start looking at me and getting better?"

She was supposed to be studying, why was she riding around on a motorcycle? There was just no way this was happening. She did have a love for motorcycles she was impressed with them.

With no helmet, there was more damage to her head than what doctors could help her with. The most severe damage was done to the brain stem. CT scans showed blood on her brain and swelling. The damage was so severe that her body's vital organs were shutting down.

*M*echanical ventilation and medications were keeping her heart beating and blood flowing to her organs. I expected Lisa's condition would improve. I saw the monitors, the blood pressure monitor; it was telling me she had blood pressure in her body, so that was good. In my mind I was telling myself she was ok and she was going to make it. In my mind I was telling the doctors she was going to wake up. I refused to believe what I was hearing and I was totally secretly telling myself what I wanted to hear. I was in shock.

There are many stories about kids and adults in serious accidents with no hope at all, and then by a miracle of god, they open their eyes and look around, then several months later they learn to stand and slowly learn how to talk again. I wanted this to be one of those stories.

I spent most of the day talking to her, holding her hand, running my fingers through her hair, just as I did when she was a little girl and she was scared or sick. How I wished she were little again. I cried and cried.

I needed the world to go back in time just 14 hours so I could change the events that took place. I felt guilty. Could I blame myself? I could blame myself for not being there. I should have at least called her on that day, maybe just minutes before she got on the bike. I would have asked "how are you"? and "what are you doing tonight"? I blame the person driving the bike. If I would have known Lisa was riding around on this bike, I would have asked questions and demanded she be safe.

For a few minutes I was actually so angry with Lisa because she made such a bad decision. Lisa did not tell me she had a friend at college who had a motorcycle. Never before had I experienced so many emotions and hatred and sadness all at one time. I was mad this all happened. I was so mad at myself.

I begged her to get better, for her to look at me. I knew time was running out, she really needed to wake up if she was going to start to get better. I kept promising her she could have anything she wanted, I would give it to her. Most of all I told her I would be more of a friend to her, listen more.

Soon her friends started calling my cell phone. They started hearing about the news. I was not sure how many different stories were going around so I was afraid to talk about it, afraid to trust them that they would respect my feelings and anger.

I felt like a criminal. Like a criminal who was shoved into a jail cell and abused. I was being sentenced to life without my daughter. I was going to go to a place where I didn't want to be. A scary, dark. lonely place.

After a while, I had to call my mom to let her know; It was very early in the morning and I didn't want to call her, she would be sad and cry. I remember her saying you mean she might not make it? crying, all I could say was "Yeah".

I called her dad. I knew it would be difficult. I did not want him to blame me or be angry with Lisa. He was compassionate but angry with the driver and the college because they did not keep her safe. I could see through the phone, he was tearing up, I could hear his voice was cracking. He offered to drive to the hospital to be with us but later I told him I would handle things and it would be better if he was at his house with his family for comfort.

It was very early in the afternoon and my mom and my brother flew in a private plane to be with us, help us sort through all this, to help us and to say goodbye. My mom helped me and as each hour passed, she held my hand tighter. She told me we would get through this. I saw her mouth move, but could not hear anything. I looked at her with a blank stare, not knowing what she meant. She helped to make phone calls to other relatives. She smiled and cried but stayed grounded to what was happening and helped me. She heard what the doctors were saying while I heard them but didn't make any sense of it.

Later on in the day at the hospital, with my mom and brother by our side, a medical doctor specialist in head injuries wanted to talk to us. He told us he had done extensive testing on my daughter's senses. He had shined a bright light into her eyes and there was no reflective response. He had slid a tube of some sort down her throat and there was no gag response. He had done a test to check if she could breathe on her own and in the 10 minutes they conducted the test she breathed on her own three times. It was confirmed a closed head injury is an injury where the skull stays intact. The neurologist explained "The rapid movement of the head can be enough to significantly injure the brain. The brain can be slammed into the inside of the skull. There is blood on her brain and swelling in the brain will follow. There was essentially no response coming from her brain, her body. State laws require doctors to do more tests and scans to be sure there are no signs of life." It was hard to sit and to look at the doctor in the face while he told me there were no responses coming from my daughter.

Then there was a conference with the medical examiner. I really did not know the whole extent of what a medical examiner did nor did I believe we were even talking to someone in this profession. Why?

He told us he examined her. I was still telling myself this wasn't that bad and did not believe what this stranger was saying to us. At that moment I heard him tell us all what we would need to take her home. I thought of all the machines we would need and how to set them up in her room. Then I heard him say we would need to call someone else home to take her home. I thought "ok, someone else can put her in their car and take her to our house." I thought this because of all the machines, a medical van with a nurse in the van would be needed in case Lisa needed medical attention on the way home.

The the stranger said something about a funeral home of your choice. Hearing this was difficult. It was not okay. What if you just let me do what I want and let me take her home?

We were then asked if we would want Lisa to have last rights. We were told there was a Chaplin onsite and he could perform this service, still not sure why, and still not wanting this and not believing I was agreeing. I let it happen because in my mind I heard we would gather by Lisa's side and pray for her to get better and be healthy. This service provided a comforting hand and helped us in remembering the good in Lisa's life and the love of their family and the legacy that she left behind. Then he left, he left us there by her side crying and saying sorry to us he left.

We were asked to sign release forms for a funeral home to have my permission to put her in a car and drive her to Wisconsin. More pain and more tears followed.

Along with all the difficult decisions there were more forms. There was a form to allow the Iowa Donor Network to donate her organs and another form to allow them to perform the surgery. This was the last surgery of all; it's what Lisa wanted.

At the end of the day it was time for us to leave the hospital. This was a real separation, the whole accident, her injuries and knowing she was not able to come with us was awful. It was all coming to surface and I was not ready. It was hard to leave; it was the longest journey I ever took, walking away, down the hallway of the hospital, out the door. With what? Wanting to run back to her I kept walking, I knew if I ran back to her I would not leave and the staff would have to pry my hands from her. I no longer had my heart; I no longer had the biggest part of me. I had a hole and nothing to fill it with. Nothing made sense. I was thinking I missed so many chances to love her more, hug her more and to thank her more.

The University of Dubuque held a prayer memorial the next day so the students could have time to reflect and pray. It was a beautiful service, we all cried so much. All of her college friends wanted a chance to remember. They all wanted the opportunity to honor her and celebrate.

We attended a luncheon and after we went to her dorm to pack her belongings. Everything we packed a few weeks earlier we now had to pack up again. Some of those things were still in boxes and books she bought never opened. With my mom and my brother in Lisa's car, we drove back to Wisconsin. It was a horribly sick silent ride. My face was wet and my eyes puffy.

In a note from UD dance instructor Deanne Hohmann she shared that, … "the past few weeks Lisa rallied a group of girls together for a dance team of which she is the captain. She held practices Monday, Wednesday, and Friday at 6:45 a.m. In addition, she has served as a resident assistant in Cassat Hall and is highly regarded by the students with whom she lives and works. In both of these ways, she exemplified the student leadership, which we, as a University, prize. In the twelfth chapter of Hebrews, we are reminded that those who have gone before us surround us in a huge cloud of witnesses to the life of faith and we are challenged to run with endurance the race that God has set before us. Lisa has joined the Spartan section of that cloud of witnesses that now cheers each of us on in our race. We honor her and Grant before her by dedicating our lives to running our race with care, love, compassion, and service to others. Now we return Lisa to Him who has known her before she was born, trusting again in God's unfailing mercy and care."

When we got home my dad was waiting for us, crying. He helped unload the boxes. All the boxes were put silently in Lisa's room then we closed the door. The next day my dad talked to me about decisions I had to make. Flowers, the funeral and a lawyer. A lawyer? I didn't even know how to get a lawyer. He also said we would have to meet with the pastor of our church to discuss what would happen during the service.

It was the furthest thing from my mind. Why? I couldn't. I still wasn't settled on her not being here. I was forced to do this. It took everything I had to do this. If my dad had not come over, I would have not done anything.

In the next few days, lots of people stopped by the house. There were neighbors, friends and relatives, all bringing things to eat, and little gifts. We as a family wanted to be together; but I was not very social at this time. Everyone was letting us be. Certain people I felt had more rights to come over and hang out than other people did. But whoever came over they had a specific reason. It helped them to help us.

I noticed there was not any time for me to cry on anybody's shoulder, as people were busy with making plans. The high school cheerleader coach came by with Lisa's high school cheerleader team colleagues. They wanted to make a collage of pictures to display at her service. I called it a remember me party. Remember me party's happened several times after that.

Lisa's service was beautiful. Almost 800 people attended. There was singing, and friends and family reading their sweet memories of her.

The Theresa Firefighter's all attended in Class A uniforms from head to toe. I was very surprised and felt so proud. After the service, the Theresa Firefighters were the first ones out, Eric and the EMTS carried Lisa out, then Lisa's immediate family. When we all got to the doors of the church, the Theresa Firefighters honored Lisa saluting with one arm and with their other arm held their swords up.

A steady stream of hundreds and hundreds of people have been coming into the sanctuary to pay their respects to a beautiful young woman who captured the attention of those around her with the ease and glory of a monarch butterfly shining on a milkweed in the noonday sun.

It is a senseless tragedy, a terrible loss that no words can take away. Like everyone else I know who knew Lisa, I can't think of her except as one of those people who convinces you that we live in a wonderful world because there are people like Lisa in it.

Lisa lit up whatever room she entered. She wore her heart of gold on the outside, for all to see. I cannot forget her love of life and empathy for everyone.

Lisa's life was short, but it was full. She knew how to get the most out of everything. She made things happen. She knew how to get her way. She seized the day.

Lisa was born to be a princess, and she was. She loved glitter and gloss and whenever she wore a crown, a tiara, you knew it was meant for her.

Lisa always needed to know that other people loved her, and as long as she knew that, she was happy.

She was a leader, a great bosser, always thinking of things to do and getting people to do them. She excelled in everything she did.

Our church started a food pantry the high school quickly pitched in and made the food pantry and the Compassionate Fund part of its mission. Lisa was one of the school's first representatives on the Board of Directors. She was a mover-and-shaker and got other students involved. Whenever we talked confidentially about someone with emergency needs we wanted to help, she was all eyes and ears because she cared about everyone.

Pastor John wrote:

> *She was a leader, always thinking of things to do and getting people to do them. She excelled in everything she did. I got to know her not long after coming to Lomira three years ago. We started a food pantry here in church. The High School quickly pitched in and made the food pantry and the Compassionate Fund part of its mission. Lisa was one of the school's first representatives on the Board of Directors. She was a mover-and-shaker and got other students involved. Whenever we talked confidentially about someone with emergency needs we wanted to help, she was all eyes and ears because she cared about everyone.*

Lisa may very well have saved a man's life this summer. It was just after the floods in Fond du Lac, and the hospital was not working like it normally would. At a road construction site, a tar-making machine blew apart and a man covered with hot tar was rushed to the Emergency Room. He might have died, but Lisa, just a CNA, took charge. Supplies were lacking. She got on the Internet right away and discovered that butter might help in the situation to remove the burning tar from the man's body. So she ordered butter on the spot and the man was saved.

Lisa's patients loved her at St. Agnes. They may remember being sick and feeling terrible during their stay at the hospital. But they more likely remembered having a princess as a CNA during their stay. We have no idea, of how much good we can do just by holding someone's hand and giving them our full loving attention when they are all alone and not so sure what the future holds.

She loved hosting AFS students who came from other countries to the Lomira High School.

Ebba from Sweden wrote:

> *Of all the things we did together, prom, 4-wheeling, the dells, sleepovers and so on, it's her braiding my hair the crosses my mind the first when I think of her. She always made my hair before football games. It might sounds like a stupid little pointless memory but I loved that she always took the time to make my hair first, even when we barley new each other. I guess that sometimes the smallest things in life makes the greatest impact and that just feels like typical Lisa, she always did those small, sweet things that could just warm you up. She was also the one the taught me the most English. I knew I always could ask her how to say this, how to spell that and she would never ever make fun of me because of my mistakes. She just smiled and taught me the right way to say it, and she would help me out until I got it. I'm never going forget when she tried to teach me the difference between "ch" and "sh"... it took me forever so she composed a little rhyme that would help me out. It completely cracks me up everytime I think of it! I often think that she isn't gone, she's just in the states and I'm in Sweden and that's why we can't meet up for a girl talk. But when she doesn't answers my e-mails and she's never online it hits me, like the first time I heard about the accident, that she is actually gone and it's not the dark blue ocean that separates us anymore but the big bright sky. I miss you so much Lisa!*

She believed in community service, and while in High School, she conned other 18 year olds into coming to church whenever a Blood Drive was going on. She gave blood and so did they.

When Lisa asked you to do something, it was hard to turn her down. Her enthusiasm was infectious. Shannon Stein, the High School Principal, said "it seems to me that a great way to honor Lisa is to make sure that from now on, all eligible 18 year olds at the High School get themselves down here every time there is a Blood Drive, and give blood. I trust that the High School will find a way to make this happen. You all know that if Lisa were put in charge of doing it, she would make it happen. Now it's up to you. She can and will live on through your response to this invitation".

There is a passage in the Bible most of us have heard, and it goes like this: "Unless a grain of wheat falls into the ground and dies, it remains alone; but if it dies, it bears much fruit." We think of Jesus when we hear this passage, as well we should. He died, and the example of his sacrificial

38

love has borne fruit ever since, challenging and inspiring people of all ages, nations, and races to live as he lived, putting the needs of others before their own. He bore our sins and contradictions in a way he alone could do.

But this passage also applies to Lisa. She died, and her heart soon thereafter went to save the life of someone. Her lung saved someone else, and it won't be long before her kidneys and liver may save someone else's life. Once again, you say you love Lisa. That's why you are here. Well, prove it. Don't be an idiot. Sign up to be an organ donor. You too may save a life and be a hero.

"Someday I will wish upon a star." Lisa loved that phrase. She had it tattooed on her foot. At the University of Dubuque, at the chapel service in her memory, her friends wore t-shirts with that phrase, and Lisa's name on the back."Someday I will wish upon a star." Lisa was a star. She is a star, and if you have eyes to see, you will be able to look up at the night sky on a clear, cold winter's night, and you will see her twinkle in the dark. "Today, our community is called to come together as we mourn the passing of one of the University's luminous lights, Lisa Martin.

On my birthday March 1 2008, 6 months before the accident, she took me out to dinner. We went to Red Lobster and she let me order whatever I wanted. It was the best day of my life.

In September 2008, two weeks before the tragedy, she drove to Wisconsin to visit as she did quite often. She spent time talking and gathering things out of her room and reminded me in less than 7 months, she would be turning 20 years old. She was very excited. I was too but it was all to soon. That was the last time we saw her alive.

Lisa was found of poofy dresses. She and a friend went shopping one night to find one for an upcoming dance at school and she found this big, red, sparkly dress. It was expensive but she had to have it. She called me from the shop and asked if she could have the money to get it. I said I would have to see it first so the very next night we went to the shop and I saw this amazing red, big poofy dress. She tried it on and showed it off to me to prove she looked beautiful in it so I would get it for her. After hours of talking and looking at it, I called her dad. I told her to ask her dad for some money and I would put a down payment on this dress. Soon the dress was hers, she was so happy and she looked just beautiful.

One day, months afterward, I turned on her laptop computer. I found all kinds of pictures and videos. There were many pictures of her friends but mainly there were pictures of her. I looked at them until everything on the screen turned blurry; several weeks later I would turn on the laptop again and look at more things.

I found pictures of wedding cakes and wedding dresses. With all the wedding reception places in Chicago and the surrounding suburbs, there were so many options. Beautiful and unique banquet facilities, excellent gourmet menus. She would have had every detail sparkle and shine.

She would have looked just amazing like no other. She wanted a fairy tale wedding and just like Cinderella, to be driven off in a horse and carriage.

Every little girl dreams of her wedding day, when she is a princess for a day in a beautiful white gown. Her gown would have transformed her into the princess she always wanted to be. Her hair in big flowing curls. The groom and groomsmen in tux coats and possibly top hats. She would have had a beautiful first dance with her handsome groom. Her groom twirling and dipping her. I know for a fact she would have included a horse drawn carriage.

Lisa in a red poofy dress

Grieving takes time. This is not going to happen overnight. Grieving is personal and can depend on a variety of things. People can grieve over not just the death of a loved one but also a loss of a job. A person may be sad at first, then happy after a couple of weeks, then go back to being sad.

I am lonely and sad and at least 1 day a month I do nothing but cry. Nighttime is the worst. I close my eyes to sleep but see Lisa. I say a prayer every night and thank her for looking over me and protecting me. I thank her for helping me. I go to sleep with tears on my pillow. Some nights are worse than others. Once I start crying I can't stop.

I didn't know there were stages of grieve until I went through it myself.

Denial, I was in denial that the accident itself was not as bad as the doctors were telling me. Even though the whole time the doctors faces were sad, concerned and not inviting.

Anger, yes I am angry and still am angry.

Bargaining, I still bargain but not as often. Bargaining with the powers that be to turn things around and make time go backwards, oh how I wish I had the power to go back in time. I wish I had the power to make her well and have her here with me.

Depression yes, I am depressed. Sometimes with a smile and sometimes with laughter.

Acceptance, have I accepted it? No, I haven't.

I am sad because I did not get to tell Lisa all the things I wanted her to know. I want to make sure she still loves me and thinks about me. I have learned she is being loved and cared for by spiritual guardians. She is learning and growing in heaven, and she wants me to grow now so I can be bigger in heaven with her. I have learned physical life is to learn how to love completely, including yourself.

Everyday I imagine what my daughter is doing and how she is going about her work. I also think about the moment she left us. What did she experience? How did she feel? Did she think about me? Did she think about what would happen to me if she went away forever? I feel like she might have stayed if she knew all the crying and heartache this would cause me.

I have read a person leaves their body and enters a room where they observe what's being done to them. What if Lisa had made the decision to come back? Could she? Did she want to? Why didn't she? I had found myself angry with her for not coming back to me. Didn't she see how upset I was? Didn't she care? I wanted her to do me this favor and come back as if nothing ever happened.

What were her first thoughts when she entered the most amazing place? I know there was a bright light not blinding, beautiful luminous light the joy and awesomeness is beyond words. There is a great deal of happiness and peace.

I know there is no sense of time; time is not measured like it is on earth. I know she understands more, more meanings, more maturity. It's a celebration. Lisa loved celebrations, whether she was helping out with the celebration, or she was the main attraction she was there.   I believe she was welcomed more graciously than she ever thought she could. I know she spent some time getting to know her new surroundings before she was given a project to do.

Life is different in heaven, people are different. She is the center of god's love and he is the center of hers. I imagine her having lots of friends and their joy will be loud in laughter. There is singing, rejoicing and storytelling, relaxation, leisure and freedom. I imagine there is wisdom and beauty all around her. Peace and pure love comes to her. She is taking time to notice all of the wonders of this place, enjoying it, living it.

I have learned, your loved ones visit maybe quite often at first, then they back away and let your life go on. They leave you to help you, they do not desert you. They still are with you and visit you in your deepest sleep.   I have learned my loved one may be having just as hard time with accepting their passing as I am. I have to respect her process just as people have to respect mine. If I pull to hard, it will make it harder for her to move on, and I don't want to do that. I can't ask her to help me cope, I need help.

I have read that having loved ones visit in dreams is common. I have had dreams with Lisa in them, they were all sad but wonderful. I welcome these dreams, and really want to have visits from her every night but it does not happen.

My first dream was of me visiting her college and her giving me the grand tour. She wanted so badly for me to visit her and for me to like the college she chose. We took our time visiting all the rooms in the school, talking and smiling. All the time she was wondering why her friends were not calling her on her cell phone. She looked amazing. At first she had on jeans and a green shirt, as the dream neared the end, she wore a bright white dress. The dream came to an end, and she asked me if she had to leave and I said yes, she faded in and out, and then walked through this wall of bright light. I remember feeling lifted, but sad too. In the morning and that day, I was sad; it was like going through the whole hearing of the news of the accident again.

Another dream I had was of her in the hospital sick and injured but getting up and doing nurses duties. As the dream went on, she worked; she felt better and looked better. The dream ended the same as the first.

Another dream I had was of her and Jacob. She and Jacob were both the same age, and drinking milk out of baby bottles. They played and smiled and they talked as if they were 20-year-old adults.

I am not alone in wishing my daughter would visit me more often. I cry and pray just like others do.

I had a dream a few days after her 22nd birthday in 2011. I dreamed I received a message by an older lady to take a trip to a corn field in some far away dry state. I had specific instructions on how to get to this place and what to do when I get there. I was to walk on this long country road, to a cabin. I had to arrive at a certain time and wait for further instructions.

When I got there, the lady said her name was Phyllis and showed me to my room. I suddenly had this overwhelming knowledge of why I was there. Lisa had called me to come, not directly, she contacted Phyllis and Phyllis contacted me.

I then knew I was waiting for Lisa to come to this cabin to visit with me. Lisa would not enter the cabin as it was not allowed, so I had to sit on a chair along side of the road and wait for her to come out of the fields. I could only sit in a chair and wait for her when it was a certain time of the day and only after Phyllis felt Lisa and I were ready. I could only stay out there for a couple of hours.

I had been at the cabin for some time when Phyllis gave me the ok to go to the road and sit in the chair and wait. It took a couple of nights, each night going out at the same time and having to come in at the same time. Finally, I went out to the chair as I was told, and it happened.

Lisa floated out of the corn field, sat on my lap and we talked and smiled at each other for a while, then she told me to be out here again the next night, and I was. We had three nights of me sitting in the chair, Lisa sitting on my lap, and us smiling. Then I had to leave and go home as there was limited time. After I woke up it was clear to me why I had this dream and what it meant so I was very happy. Most importantly the timing of the dream. I told my mom about this dream because the message was to emphasize what she has been telling her kids and grand kids their whole lives and that is "you will never be too old to sit in my lap".

I thank her every time I have a dream or a visit from her. I tell her I love her and miss her every night. Most dreams are the Lord's way of healing us. It's a good thing; it shows us our loved one is just fine. We have to heal and this is one way the Lord does it. They are showing us they are happy and want us to be happy for them. If we have enough strength, we can be happy, at times our strength seems to fail us, so we worry, cry or are angry.

It helps me to read other people's stories and experiences. I get teary eyed at times, and then have to do something else for a while. I do find out some answers to my questions and maybe a resolution. I like to read the amazing stories for inspiration and hope.

"Just that it was our time, God has called and said "come live with me now". On the other side of goodbye, the sun does shine, the flowers do grow, and the water does flow. The memory of the person who's gone still remains, and when we are on the other side with them the pain grows smaller, we are healed." http://www.generations.on.ca/teen-grief.htm

I think about what if I were enter God's house, his kingdom? How would I feel? I think I would understand things more clearly, I would learn from him. I would want to learn everything God has to teach me, I would obey. I know I would be overcome with joy and love.

I know people are going to meet me and take my hand. I think as soon as someone touches my hand, the impurities will dissolve. I will never know what sweetness is until this moment, I will never know how beautiful the woods and the oceans are till I am there with God. My steps will be soft and fluffy. I will swiftly move without falling. The water will fall around me, cleanse me, but not wash me away. The sun will shine brightly but not blind me.

Lisa had a damaged body when she left, one that would not have been well enough to sustain life. She would be in so much pain now. Now, I am taking on pain, she is living pain free, I am working through the bills and putting up with life, she is living rent-free and having new life run through her. I will live through this darkness for her because I know her world would be dark.

"There will be bright days of warm colors shining on me when I am with her. I know she wouldn't have wanted me to live through such pain and suffering. She wants me to stop crying. She is very much alive in my heart; I must stop and hear her voice whispering in my heart." http://www.recover-from-grief.com

I have noticed she is sending messages to me at certain times. I smell her perfume. I know it's her and I usually try to say something out loud to her. For months after her accident, I thought I heard the telephone ring at odd times 1 or 2 in the morning. It would ring and ring then stop. Sometimes I could actually feel her talking to me, I felt this awesome light air, calmness and happy joyous feeling. It was a real sense of reassurance. I always have wanted more though. I have to stop with wanting it so bad. I find this is the hardest thing to do. How can I give up? I have prayed out loud and shouted asking her to please come visit me and it doesn't work. I must learn more how to be patient.

I try not to bring anyone else down by talking about my feelings or talk about what kind of a day I am having. I am feeling anger and sadness and am told not to let it consume me but sometimes I want it to. Anybody asks how I am doing I say good but inside I hurt. I really do not know what they mean when they ask me that question. When some of my friends find out I am having a bad day they ask what's wrong, I think for sure they would know why.

The sadness can be overwhelming and consumes me. I feel pain in my neck, shoulders and in my heart. I start to cry and the tears keep coming, they don't stop. After a while my head hurts and my eyes are puffy.

At times I do want to talk, I want to reach out, but how do I start the conversation? Do I say, "hey I was wondering if you had a minute?" But then I think "well why bother them?" they all have lives. I am about to trust my friend with my feelings, feelings they do not know or feel. Can I? Are they strong enough? And after I reveal how I am feeling, what is going to be their response? I know it's not going to be the response I am looking for. I usually want someone else to make the first move. Someone to reach out to me, ask me" how are you doing today?" I won't bore you with all these crying episodes I am having, or all the sleepless nights and I won't take up too much of your time because I know you have a full schedule already.

Sometimes when I am online, I initiate a conversation. I am always the first one who says "hi". I feel like I am knocking on a door with people standing behind it trying to be as quiet as possible, I know people are there online, I can see their names, but they don't answer. The chat box appears and I always start out with "hi". I get nothing back. I wait for a "hi" back or "how are you"? Still nothing.

I understand Lisa's friends are not my friends. At the time when they were younger, they needed rides to friends houses, to the movies, to the mall and out to eat, I drove them. I didn't complain. At the time, they needed to talk to someone, a person who just could listen and not be told what to do, I was there. I miss those conversations. I am surprised I do not hear from Lisa's friends, I thought I would. Sometimes I want people to stop what they are doing and ask me how I am doing, to think about me.

I do what I can for other people. I am there to listen and I like that about myself. I hope to give people strength when they are struggling with life. If I am asked for an opinion I may give it in the tenderness of my heart. I understand the frustrations but cannot tell them what to do.

Oh sure I smile, laugh and have a good time, I have my son and my husband who need me and we have a great time together. I don't ruin our good times by crying, I just have fun. Just because I'm smiling doesn't mean I am happy, I am often silent when really I am screaming inside.

Family time is more important to me now more than ever. If there is ever a time when I have a chance to spend time with family, I will do it. I will make vacation plans, and ask for time off from work, if the workplace has a problem with it, then I would put my foot down and express how important family time is to me, then whatever happens, happens as I will be with my family.

I have talked to the driver of the bike. It seems he and Lisa were friends for a short while. I told him I am angry with him. I wanted him to hear it from me. As I sat there he could not look me in the eyes. I was at a loss for words. I could not look the driver in the eyes and tell him everything is ok. I was so mad I couldn't talk. This young college boy could never come close to knowing the pain. He doesn't know what pain is. I wish he could know the pain of the crying I do.

The night of the accident, Lisa took her friend out for his birthday. This is what he wrote 3 days later:

"So we went to Brick town and had an amazing dinner, and after we ate we just sat there and talked for what seemed like forever… we talked about everything from your family, how much you cared about Eric, and even about how much you love stars… you even told me that I should get a star tattoo and I told u that you were… crazy… so you held out my hand and drew a tiny blue star on the back of it with a pen… a star that will last forever now because I got it traced over and permanently tattooed in the same color blue ink right where you drew it.

After we left I thanked you for giving me the best birthday ever and all you said was "good, I cant wait to do it next year!" those words now tear me apart because I know that is now impossible. I am so sorry and I apologize to you and to everyone that the night ended as tragically as it did. There is nothing that I wouldn't give to be able to bring you back and trade you places."

On the days he has to celebrate, I want him to feel pain. When all his family gets together to celebrate some big accomplishment or a holiday I want him to be sad. I hope next time he gets on or near a bike, he shakes with fear and starts to cry. I hope he does not just get back on a bike, and drive away.

*S*ince *the accident happened in* Iowa, and all the emergency procedures were done in Iowa, the hospital had counselors on site to help us. They also had a team to contact the Donor Network so they could come in and talk to us and ask us if we would be interested and willing to donate organs. The Medical team is separate from the transplant team to ensure all efforts will be made to save a life before organ donation is considered.

The transplant team fully explained the donation process to us and we were assigned an independent donor advocate who made sure of our rights and would be our contact.

For the first year, information about the recipients and our information was kept confidential. We did get a letter from the Iowa Donor Network telling us the recipients sent a thank you letter and wanted to know if it would be ok if it was sent to us, we agreed, and when I replied, I sent a letter with a picture of Lisa. I sent all my letters and pictures to the Iowa Donor Network and then they forwarded it to the recipients.

A year passed and her roommate and best friend, Kellie held a Donation Awareness Night in memory of Lisa. It had been the first time I visited the college since the accident. I remember walking into the gymnasium and seeing the huge crowd. All the banners said WELCOME TO DONATION AWARENESS NIGHT IN MEMORY OF LISA MARTIN. There were easels with pictures of Lisa everywhere and also with every organ there was an easel of the recipient's information on it. Kellie planned the whole night, it was amazing. She even arranged to have Lisa's heart recipient and her lung recipient attend. Kellie planned to have the UD dance team Lisa formed, to dance. It had special meaning. So during the half time of the boys basketball game, Kellie had Lisa's recipients down on the floor, and introduced them to the crowd. Then the dance team danced. It was all so perfect and Kellie cried so much. The night was incredible. I had met two of Lisa's recipients. I was able to talk to them and take pictures. Even after our family met the recipient's families, I still did not get it but it will come with time.

I have kept in contact with Lisa's lung recipient and her heart recipient and have become somewhat close. I have their numbers stored in my phone and have their addresses in my phone book. I like to hear how they are doing. I like it when I read in their letters, that they are out fishing or hunting, back to doing the things they love to do again. I have also asked if they would write what this whole experience was like for them.

Lung Recipient:
Marla, Marv's wife and Marv wrote:

During Thanksgiving in 1999, Marv had what appeared to be a bad cold. A cough accompanied this cold. It continued so he went to his doctor and he said it was congestive heart failure and referred him to his cardiologist. Marv had already had triple by pass heart surgery in 1994 so he had a heart specialist.

The heart doctor told him it wasn't heart failure and just thought it was walking pneumonia and didn't seem to concerned. Meanwhile the coughing continued. Marv went back to his doctor. Eventually he was sent to see a lung specialist. The lung specialist did breathing tests and gave him pills to take, all the time his coughing continued.

He went to another lung doctor and this one has been with him ever since. This doctor stuck a scope down his throat and flushed his lungs, this showed 1 spore of Farmer's lung which is a disease but it was determined this was not a problem with just having 1 spore. Marv continued to see his doctor and his cough and lungs were getting worse.

Lung Recipient: Marv

Then in 2003, after still getting nowhere, the doctors did a lung biopsy, which determined he had Idiopathic Pulmonary Fibrosis. He was put on a chemo medicine, which was very hard on his body and teeth.

In the last part of 2003, Marv was sent to confer with the head of the lung department at Iowa City. He was very negative and basically told Marv he was going to die and had already lived longer than what was normal for the disease.

Marv is a very strong willed and determined person and it made him angry that any doctor would be so unkind. Marv was determined to prove the doctor wrong. At this time they were not doing lung transplants in Iowa City.

He continued to see his doctor and at one point she admitted she did not think he was going to live to the end of 2003 for his appointment in December.

In 2004, Marv's doctor told him of a lung trial for IPF that they were doing in Iowa City and she wanted him to try to get in that. After many trips and tests, Marv was received into this trial. This trial continued for 2 years and during this time he seemed to be doing better but the awful coughing never stopped.

Time seemed to be running out for him and soon he was put on oxygen when he slept. We talked about selling our acreage as we were having a hard time keeping it up.

In 2008, Marv went to his appointment with his doctor and she mentioned transplant. It shocked him as they had said earlier; they didn't do them in Iowa City. Marv talked it over with the rest of the family and said they would go with whatever decision he made. Transplant was scary, but on the other hand we knew he wouldn't survive without one.

The doctor sent all his records to Iowa City and in March of 2008, we visited the transplant team. Marv was put on oxygen 24 hours a day now, which was a hard thing to accept for a while until he realized it had to be and was willing to do anything to get a new lung.

The choice involved many tests, as they want to make sure you are strong enough to survive the transplant and have an organ donated not to be used. He also found out he would only get one lung due to the bi pass heart surgery.

On July 15th 2008, Marv was officially put on the list and they told him he needed one very soon.

On the morning of September 19th Marv received the call telling him they thought they had a compatible lung for him, but would keep in touch. We arrived about 2:00pm in Iowa City, surgery started about 7:00pm, and ended at about 11:00pm.

We never knew who donated the lung until you wrote back to us. That is all kept very confidential, as some donor families never seem to get in touch. Several of the transplants that we know have never heard from their donor families, even though they have written to them.

Words will never convey the gratefulness we feel toward Lisa for her choice of organ donation, but again we have the sorrow for you, her family that you had to lose her for Marv to have a whole new life. Marv tries to follow all the things the doctors tell him to do to protect the precious gift that Lisa gave him because it has given him so much of his old life back and he has experienced very few of the problems you can experience with transplants. He had experienced little rejection early on but they regulated the meds for that.

In closing we continue to think of you and your family, you will always be special to us and are so glad you chose to write back and meet us and are so thankful for the gift of the lung and to our powerful God who allowed Marv to continue with life until he was able to receive the lung.

Heart Recipient:
Monica, Rod's wife and Rod wrote:

> Rod's health problems started in August of 2003, at the age of 47, when he had a massive heart attack that destroyed 75% of his heart. There was enough damage that no stints or bypass options were available so a balloon pump was installed to help his heart regain what little function it could.
>
> When it came time to remove the pump, it proved more difficult than they thought and he was sent to the University of Iowa Hospitals and Clinics to be evaluated for a heart transplant. They concluded that a regime of medication would work and that he did not need a transplant. So he was given the medication and that all worked pretty well until March of 2006 when he had a defibrillator put in to try and regulate his heart rhythm.

Heart Recipient: Rod

All went well again until March of 2008 when his health began to decline at a pretty rapid pace. An update to a pacemaker/defibrillator was put in but his heart continued to stay in atrial fibrillation—irregular heartbeats. So he then had an AV node ablation (severing the top part of the heart from the bottom) in hopes that it would put his heart back into a normal rhythm again. This did not happen. He continued to be in the hospital for about a week each month as the pressure in his lungs remained high and blood flow was a problem.

At the beginning of September, the blood flow was so low that his organs were being compromised and were at the beginning stages of shutting down. A heart transplant was his only option so the work up for that began. In anticipation of a long wait time, Rod was scheduled to get an LVAD (left ventricle assistance device), or heart pump to help him bridge the gap until a heart became available. Due to the amount of time required to stay in the hospital after such a surgery, (at least one month) the decision was made to put in a pic-line (kind of a permanent IV line) and he was able to come home on that medication to get things in order until the time of the surgery, scheduled for September 22, 2008.

You are well aware of what happened then—one week after officially being put on the transplant list and four days before that LVAD surgery, a heart became available.

The doctors said that Lisa's heart was a perfect match for Rod—size and tissue type as well as blood type all lined up. They told us that usually they call in a second patient in case it doesn't work for the first one, but with this case, they didn't even do that, it was such a perfect fit. The surgery was about six hours long and when I got to see him in the recovery room, he had color for the first time in a very long time. He was in the surgical intensive care for four days, then he moved down to the heart care floor for four more days and then we were discharged to a local hotel where we had to stay for another week before being allowed to come home. He recovered very quickly with no problems at all—it indeed was a perfect fit.

As you can probably tell—there are a ton of tests that are run before you are even considered for a transplant. There cannot be anything wrong, other than the organ in question, because of the medications you are given for rejection. They are hard on your kidneys and would accelerate any cancer cells. So you are definitely given a battery of tests and run through the mill.

Rod used to work as a jeweler and watchmaker, is trained in that area but for the last fifteen years he has worked in a factory, most recently in inventory control. He was a coach for his kids when they were in T-ball and football. He liked to work outside in the yard and keep it looking nice. When he had his heart attack, that all changed.

He just didn't have the energy to do much, would get short of breath and his whole demeanor changed. Right before the transplant, he couldn't even walk 50 feet without stopping to rest. Hard to take for someone who used to be pretty active. He had to go to part time in the months leading up to the transplant and in the middle of August, had to stop completely.

After the transplant, he was off work for a year, and then allowed to return, first on a part-time basis and then full time. He continues to work full time.

While not completely shocked, we were surprised that he had gotten to the point of needing a heart transplant. We thought we could just change medications and it would be fine—but it didn't turn out that way. When the doctor told us, I cried but Rod was really a trooper—I really don't think I could have gone through all he has. When we got the call that a heart was available, Rod was so excited and happy—he was so sure that everything would work out and of course he was right—I was happy for him but broke down because we had just been through so much in recent months. This was the only call we received—he had never been told that he would not get a heart.

You like to think that you would but you never know! He still has to go through things since the transplant—they constantly monitor for rejection and adjust his meds according to blood tests. Some people have told him that they would not want to do what he has to do and wouldn't have received a transplant—he just tells them that you do what it takes in order to not die.

The Iowa Donor Network works in combination with the heart failure nurses at UIHC and so we didn't actually talk to them. They cannot tell us anything about the donor and so we knew nothing, only that it was a young heart. But boy did we wonder! We went to the offices of the network to leave the card we sent you and the lady who took it didn't say much—only that she knew you would be very happy to know that Rod was doing so well.

They are very good at guarding the identity of the donor family, as they should be.

When we received your first packet, with the letter and pictures of Lisa, it was the same day a benefit was being held for us by Rod's company. We took her pictures to the benefit and displayed them on a table so everyone there could see what a beautiful girl had done for someone she would never meet! She became one of our family that day and has been one ever since! As a matter of fact, our youngest daughter was having to do a family tree presentation in her Spanish class today, and she took Lisa's picture so she could include her in it.

This book is dedicated to those who have lost a child. It is dedicated to the families.

I think about what Lisa would be doing now if she were here. I know she would have a job in a hospital, as a head nurse. She probably would be married and maybe expecting her own bundle of joy. She would be keeping up with her studies and may be in college. She would be keeping up with all the gossip from her friends and would continue to spread herself thin to make sure she spends time with everyone she loves.

So many loved, so many lost, now all we have are the memories. We need to keep close to those memories and the love, never lose it. Smile and remember them.

I think what if Lisa hadn't died in the accident; she would be in a wheel chair with machines. She would not be able to open her eyes, breathe on her own, talk or probably not even be able to swallow. There are so many things in life she enjoys; she would not like to live if she would not fully be able to do all of those things. If she needed help with any of the personal basic life skills, I think she would be sad she could not do them herself.

Lisa's favorite flower was the Calla lily. The Calla lily symbolizes purity, faith, youth and innocence many of which I have made references to in this book. I have made several references to Hope.

The story of Eric is true and full of hope; we hoped Eric's cancer would just leave so he could live his life without pain. Cari, Eric's wife wrote, "I can not wait for the day when I come home from work, and there's a healthy, happy Eric waiting for me. It will be the happiest day of my life when I get to bust him out of this hospital for what I am calling his last cancer treatment, and into our home, so we can start decorating, having kids, and building our lives together."

We all prayed and hoped for Lisa's full recovery. We all cried. We all hope Lisa's friends will live life to the fullest, I hope for them to be successful and happy. We hoped the recipients of Lisa's organs would be healthier and it would truly make a difference in their lives.

Rod's family and Marv's family hoped they would get healthier. They prayed for and felt many kinds of emotions. They pondered all the options; organ donation was furthest from their minds. They both were being educated on what options they did have which mainly consisted of medications. They communicated to their families of what was needed and the possible outcomes. Hoping the medications would do the trick.

Spend time with your children, play with them, hug and kiss them everyday. Tell them you love them, it won't be too long and they will be out on their own and will be busy with their own things.

If your child wants another push on the swing, or another scoop of ice cream just give it to them.

One of Lisa's favorite things was the swing at the park. I wish I could go back in time so I could give her more pushes on the swing.

Lisa's favorite quote:
Dance as though no one is watching you.
Love as though you have never been hurt before.
Sing as though no one can hear you.
Live as though heaven is on earth.
~Souza

Lisa on a swing

Like the stars in the sky,I am calling to you. From the heavens above,I am looking for you.In the depths of my soul,I will live and breathe for you.Sadness dwells inside you;You have nothing to fear,for I am next to you.I can feel your sadness;Let me be sad for you,so you will feel love once again.Worry not about life,let me worry for you. You should always love life,for it is a part of you.I'll be there when you fall,to catch you and say I Love You...

Author Unknown